Don Marcelino's Daughter

September 2005

David

Don Marcelino's Daughter

Tim Cunningham

With thanks for sharing
a wonderful week.
 Best of luck with the
poetry & studies.
 Tim

PETERLOO POETS

First published in 2001
by Peterloo Poets
The Old Chapel, Sand Lane, Calstock, Cornwall PL18 9QX, U.K.

**A catalogue record for this book is available
from the British Library**

ISBN   1-871471-89-3

Reprinted 2004

Printed and bound in Great Britain by
Antony Rowe Ltd, Chippenham and Eastbourne

ACKNOWLEDGEMENTS

Acknowledgements are due to the editors of the following publications in which some of these poems appeared for the first time: *Ambit, Bad Poetry, Borderlines, The Countryman, Cyphers, Dandelion, Encounter, Envoi, The Honest Ulsterman, The Irish Times, Iron, Moonstone, New Irish Writing (The Irish Press), Orbis, Other Poetry, Poetry Ireland Review, Sol, The Times Literary Supplement, The Turner Society News.*

for ...
Alex
Eve and Alan

Contents

Stones

We played on the Treaty Stone's steep
Steps, slippery with history and rain.

We knew the tales of Ginkel and of Sarsfield,
Of heroic defence and sails too

Late appearing up the Shannon.
But all we wanted was to climb,

To be king of the King John's castle,
Little Arthurs tugging at Excaliburs.

Fingers learning the braille of stone
Was incidental, a bonus for exile

When gulls, not wild geese, spread
Wings on Dun Laoghaire and Rosslare

Tides. Touching the Hepworths in St.
Ives or the monolithic Moores

Beside the Thames is recognition,
A triggering of instinct. And the name is right:

'Mór', translated 'big' or 'huge';
Like the Treaty Stone, like a child's imagination.

Map

'This is Ireland,' the teacher said,
Outlining the mystery in white
Chalk. It seemed playful;
A shaggy pup learning to beg,
High-wiring on fifty one
And a half degrees North latitude.
Gradually we filled in the features:
The Mizen Head and Baltimore
Hind legs, the puppy fat
Sagging from the Clare coastline,
The Lough Neagh eye, the Ards
Peninsula flapping
Like a Strangford ear, the solid
Meath and Wicklow back
Scrubbed by the Irish Sea. We learned
A little of its history, of its 'merry
Wars and sad songs.' So I imagined
The Mourne Mountains, Galtees
And Twelve Pins as weals and lesions
From Viking axes and Norman
Spears, and saw the Moy trickle
Like a tear. But the teacher countered
That the braille of its hills and mountains
Was too beautiful for this reading,
Suggested that famine, intrigue,
Massacres and wars were fleas
In the country's soft, resilient
Coat. In time we knew perspective,
Saw it in relation to the rest
Of the world, observed that its longitude
String did not dangle from another
Finger, noticed its Carnsore
Tail wagging at England,
Its Malinmore nose
Sniffing Atlantic salt,
Its Connemara and Mayo paws
Reaching for America's hand.

The Straw Bonnet

A halo of flowers circles the bonnet
Behind a New England door

Trophied in spring and summer with daisies,
Lilac, tulips, crocuses,
Hyacinth, cythia, flowering quince
And ribbons of white and blue.

With autumning leaves, fall colours succeed:
Oranges, golds and browns
Burning from chrysanthemums, marigolds, dried
Wheat, maple leaves and Indian

Corn until winter buries this excess
In a red-green wreath of pine sprigs,
Berries, cones, even snowmen, birds
And bows, and sometimes ever

Green rushes like the rushes behind
A Limerick door, matted
To a perfect St. Brigid's cross and nailed
With the horseshoe and prayer to St. Kevin

Assuring the widow that, with any luck,
She is cantering towards heaven.

The Corbally Plot

Little and of little
Help, I followed between drills,
Lobbing my feet

Precisely on the polished
Prints his brown town
Shoes mapped

On earth like stones
Across a stream. Sometimes
He allowed me tuck

The split potato
In behind his levered
Shovel then sealed

His tiny treasure
In a vault of soil. Another
Day he would pause

To 'cut his smoke'
And offer me his blunt
Tobacco knife

To sink from seven
Paces in the belly of a tree.
Retracting that old

Blade, it seemed
Somehow as if a wound was healed.
And my hand found

Something in those rough
Clay pockets that has weathered
Frost and drought.

Hallowe'en

My father's absence was always there
At Christmas, birthdays and hallowe'en
When molten lead through an iron key
Shaped futures in a shallow basin.

Cargoes of exotic fruit
Made a treasure ship of the kitchen table
With peaches pulsing their ruby blush
And clustered grapes precious as pearls.

No Christ figure presided there,
No Judas to sell us short, no John.
And how would Leonardo paint
A candle hurting for its flame?

His Letter

Opening the letter,
Words flew up like butterflies,
Exploded with rainbow wings.

I part the yellowing pages now
Brittle as fallen leaves;
Unbandage the past.

He writes of where he is:

Of guard duty tinselled with frost,
And stars like sixpences
Reflecting on his boyonet.

Remembers where he was:

His mother's fingers sculpting flour,
His father's feet and his
Welcome through acres of neighbouring fields.

Dreams of where he longs to be:

Alighting from the troop train,
Seeing his Venus's green coat
Appearing from a cloud of steam.

And, knowing the pencil's lead would sink
In the pages' white rapids,
He asks her to re-write his words in pen.

Then the poem's pencil-sketch of love,
Of life disappearing
Like wrens into a bush.

I read his testament,
Follow the vowel and consonantal
Roads we might have walked.

But mostly I watch her hand,
Observe it tracing faithfully
The loop and line of letters;

Her pen climbing his wordscape,
Its warm ink intimate on pencil
Like skin on skin.

Ring-Cutter

To the jeweller, a routine chore
Like taking a tin-opener
To a can. But not for her,

Watching the pike-like
Jaw trawl skin and bite
The wedding ring now tight

With tourniquets of absence and time.
Fingers of morning sunshine
Parallel a winter scene

When only the weather was cold and, standing
At the altar rails, he handed
Her silver and gold in place of the sun

And moon beyond his reach. She gives
It to the jeweller to augment and improve,
Increasing the circumference of love.

Mrs. Kirby

A protestant lived in our house.
We rented the place downstairs,
She had a room on top.
I knew she was different

Because people said she was a protestant
As if she had measles
Or came from the North Pole.
Once when we giggled in church

The woman behind said
That I was as bad as a protestant.
On Christmas Day when I was six,
A game of rings

And a huge bar of Bournville chocolate –
I remember that because it tasted
Different to a sixpenny Cadbury's –
Were slipped under our door.

My mother said that they came from Mrs. Kirby.
At last I knew what a protestant was
Though I had always thought
That Father Christmas was one of us.

Hawk

For six days the black
Hawk stooped from the cathedral
Spire, preying on chickens,

Cats, pet rabbits.
Its crucifix shadow haunted
The parish like an angel of death.

Old women in dark
Shawls blessed themselves
Like peasants in a vampire film.

Pigeons left the belfry
In a storm of feathers, never –
Says local legend –

To return. Too young
For certainties, we only knew
That the tower was one mile

High and that a rifle bullet
Travelled a mile exactly
Then dropped. So it was no surprise

When the army marksman killed
The bird with a single shot
As it perched with its back to the sun,

Its talons sunk like nails
In the cathedral cross. They say
It fell like Lucifer.

Magnolias

The sun's thin tapers
Touch magnolia wicks;
Candelabra dripping dew
Before morning's altar rich

With incense. Under a stained
Glass sky, streams bless
The foreheads of infant hills,
And acres of deep-pile grass

Spread wall-to-wall across
Sanctuary floors. Oak
And beech pillars separate
Aisles where the song thrush hops

From twig to twig like fingers
On organ keys. Hedgerows
Change their vestments with the season;
Today is cloth-of-gold.

But already stars halo chandeliers,
The moon's unleavened host shines
Its benediction, and evening's acolyte
Extinguishes magnolia flames.

'Here Be Dragons'

The king's mapmaker inks
A fleck of crimson on the world's

Cartouche, burnishes
His patron's coat of arms,

Gifts a few galleons
To the stippled sea, serpents

Spaces with bold swash letters
And, with a migratory flourish

Of quill, writes 'Here be
Dragons' on the known horizon.

On the other side, an old man
Rises from prayer to his pre-Christian

God, unfolds his goatskin
Parchment and scribbles

On the identical line:
'Here be dragon slayers.'

Errata

On the evening of the seventh day
Some ass sat on the button and annihilated
Man. God winced a little having told
The press this guy was made in His own image
And likeness and had been presented
With the crop of both sea and land for food.
So on the eighth day, being off the menu
And per se not quite so good, God blinked
And they all disappeared – just like that.
On the ninth day, the living creatures with which
The waters teemed and everything that flew
Were all gone too. By day ten the stars
And those two lights wired in the sky, really
The sun and moon, not named in Genesis
Because worshiped by local cranks, were doused.
Well, they simply had no function without
Man. The fruit and trees and plants and earth and sea
Went the same way. That was the eleventh
Day. Next day the firmament had no role
And left a vacuum like a great black hole.
On day thirteen, a Friday I believe,
God realised that without people there was
Little difference between day and night, so,
Completing the cycle, he switched off light.
Again earth was a formless void and darkness
Spread across the deep and God rested,
Rehearsing alternatives in His sleep.

St. Francis and the Birds

Suppose St. Francis got it wrong,
That his theology was mistaken
And instead of beatific visions
Death led only to reincarnation,

To his rebirth as an Assisi cat,
Back arched like a coiled spring,
Ready to pounce on a pair of sparrows
Valued, he recalls, at a farthing.

Cats' Eyes

He could go anywhere in a car
Hump across the Sahara without a radiator
Slide up Everest backwards on a single wheel
Paddle the Atlantic upside down
Even find a parking spot in Chinatown

And fascinated by the journey to heaven
He read all the books – the Bible Kama Sutra the AA Guide–
Then yesterday at noon he burned
His books and boats in the furnace of the sun

At midnight he checked his engine
Popped his dipstick in the oil
Filled up the tank with a beatific smile
And taking family and friends completely by surprise
Announced that the stars were celestial cats' eyes

Eggs for Breakfast

There is always that instant of fear
When I crack the shell,
A moment when I half expect to hear
A scream of agony and surprise
Or look into a pair of devil's eyes
Like in a fairy tale.

I wonder how my hunting heart will beat
If ever the ceiling breaks apart
And I am shovelled between teeth.

The Living Room

It has been like this since snow wrapped
Australasia in its cotton shroud
Since the disappearance of seven seas
And the silent implosion of Andes and Alps
Unhinged the balance of time

Now the floor is a flourish
Of tropical green
With bamboo shoots
Growing thick and tall
Where cane-handled umbrellas
Leaned against the wall

A snake-skin wallet
Slithers round the room
With a rattle in its tail
And a hissing on its tongue

My calf-skin boots
Are lowing for their mother
And the crocodile handbag
Behind the door
Is snapping its way
Towards a swamp once more

A fox-fur sniffs
Round the hen-house wire
And the tiger-skin leaps
From its place by the fire

Books and bookcases
Revert to trees
And the glass that I held
In the palm of my hand
Crumbles to grains
Of timeless sand

Of course the waters will return and snow
Will melt and mountains puncture cloud but when
Piano keys release again their music to the world
I know that I will hear only the trumpeting
Herds as they charge behind ivory spears

Pebbles

Like pebbles flicked
By a lover,
Stars tinkled
On the bedroom

Window. Later,
The glass shattered
And an angel in football gear
Asked politely for his moon.

Posy

I picked my love a posy
In the year two thousand and one
I picked the prettiest nettles
In the heat of the midnight sun

I chose the tallest fungi
The choicest twigs and bark
Trespassing on the precious slate
Of the metropolitan park

I plucked ragwort and thistle
Dockleaves and dandelion
Couchgrass and creeping buttercups
Bleached with acid rain

The Pharaoh's Sandals

'The Pharaoh carved two prisoners
On the soles of his sandals: one a negro,
The other an Asian from Mesopotamia.'

Reading that, the rafters of my skull
Creak with the pounding of shoes and feet:
Pheidippides, leathered in blood, announcing

Victory in Athenian streets; the Nazarene's
Insteps spiked to a tree; discalced
Palmers sanctifying roads; dancers

Tapping primeval codes; lovers
Cushioned on insoles of cloud; lice
Laced tramps; the tonal essence

Of Van Gogh's boots; slow-motion
Astronauts striding for mankind. But three
Stark images stand apart:

The farmer, the soldier and the children of war.
The farmer brought his daughter to the hospital
Door, then returned to the car for her feet.

The soldier's boot lay wedged
On a last of clay, trophied in mud
And blood; hobnailed, not star-studded.

And in Belsen and Dachau, children's shoes
Were piled in haunting pyramids. 'The Pharaoh
Carved two prisoners on the soles

Of his sandals; one a negro, the other
An Asian from Mesopotamia,' left his footprints
On the sand and sheltered from the raw sirocco.

Shuffled

Roots trailing like stalks
Of blighted crops, they disembarked
From coffin ships with nothing

But the instinct to survive.
Hearts bled, split
Like seed potatoes

Then revived in incubators
Of rich soil. Others
Flew, a phoenix

Phalanx risen
From Europe's ashes,
Covenanting

With a promising land.
Generations
Later, the skin

Itches for origins;
Fingers of ancestral
Branches beckon:

Beacons of the past.
All search prisms
For their history of light.

Home movies help,
Old albums,
Paper clippings,

Certificates of birth.
Links shimmer
Their anchor chains

In the documented tide.
And, in the dead earth
Of pogroms, in the skeletoned

Drills of famine
Fields, ghosts of old
Migrations

Hover, feathers
Spread like shuffled
Decks of cards.

'San Giorgio Maggiore, Venice'

While the osteopath's
Fingers gentled your spine,
I fingered the spines

Of his books and read
Of the Turner watercolour
Conditionally bequeathed

To Ireland's National
Gallery; its exhibition
Confined to January

Alone, presumably
To preserve its colours
And save such magical

Effects of light. Returning
To the waiting room,
Your smile a brushstroke

Of love, you sat – radiant,
Beautiful, delicate
As a watercolour.

Bathroom Venus

Something sacramental haloes the bath
A dew of isolation
In which she is her own goddess
A soft cathedral Venus
Skin luminous as lilies
Bathrobed in the sunshine's cloth-of-gold
Momentarily cleansed
Of purest love's pervasive fingerprints

Irises

From the ticket office
To the stairs
The labrador
Confidently guides

Then at the escalator top
The blind man
Gathers up his dog
Like irises

A Fistful of Daises

Because his love is certain,
The child picks fistfuls of flowers.

'Wash your hands,' his mother says,
Before spotting daisies in the chipped blue cup.

Then she beds her face in clay hands;
Plants kisses on fertile fingers.

Earrings

Her courage was twenty four
Carat, standing at the counter
In the jeweller's shop
As the June sun kindled
Trays of gold. Finally,
A clear voice speaking

From behind a mask of fear
Requested the assistant
To pierce her ears: lobes
From which to hang glass
Baubles and catch perhaps
A moonbeam or the twinkle
Of a star. Her knuckles

Whitened: a child
Just nine years
Young, but old enough
Instinctively to choose
The sudden flinch
Of pain, the fleck of blood.

Quartet

Sometimes the music stops
Sometimes Daddy's mind is resting
On the restless heaving
Of his secretary's blouse
But she knows when a heart
Is cemented in the corner of a house

Sometimes the music stops
Sometimes Mummy's hope
Is to break from the moorings
Of the kitchen sink
But love is a weighty anchor
And nothing severs the umbilical rope

Sometimes the music stops
Sometimes Junior's tongue
Is a flame
To set the world on fire
But they praise his poems
And tie him with daisy chains

Sometimes the music stops
Sometimes Sis escapes
Her schoolgirl wrapping
And dances to Svengali lights
But her spotlight is a moonbeam
On ordinary nights

Sometimes the music stops
But mostly they accept the score
And play the harmonies
That exorcise the demons at the door

Viking

Asked how the thieves broke in,
She said the patterned sails
Appeared from the mist
And the long low ships
Ran their prows up
On the beach of her doorstep.

Asked if she knew who they were,
She said they were helmeted
Warriors
Wearing mail and calling
Each other Amlav,
Magnus, Tomar.

Asked why they ransacked the room,
She said they were searching for jewels,
Enamelled
And gold trinkets,
Chalices, patens,
Ciboria.

Asked if she could be confused
About the heavy swords,
The iron spears,
The details of the crime,
She said it was merely
A matter of time.

The Etiquette of Flowers

Dressing with daffodils
His cemetery bed, she notes
How death has altered
The etiquette of flowers. Her joy

Rekindles the torch
Of his single rose; her pain resurrects
The thornprick's petal
Of blood. Leaves rustle crisp

As sheets and wedding gowns.
Then, sudden as Viking clubs,
Fists smash their history
On papyrus skin and the bag

Is ripped from her shoulder
Fiercely as cats' claws
Mauling a sparrow's
Wing. Crawling between tombstones,

Crabbing the low-tide
Styx, she finds her purse
In dead weeds; fish–
Mouth gasping with shock.

'Uitgang'

(Anne Frank House, Amsterdam)

The steep stairs rose
Like steps to a gallows.
With every breath, the anaconda
Walls crushed in.

The plateau of her room
Was airless too,
Its windows burgling
Oxygen with a sinister
Kiss. The floor was barren;
The wallpaper relieved
By photos pinned like cuttings
From a favourite garden:
'David' by Michelangelo,
Rembrandt's 'Portrait
Of an Old Man', 'The Chimps'
Tea Party', a rose
With petals white as her
Sheltered skin,
Princess Elizabeth,
Hollywood's constellation
Of Rogers, Milland,
Durbin and Greta
Garbo with crayoned
Rhododendron lips.

Descending staircases
Were tunnels to the land of the dead,
Studded with jackboot
Nightmares, the ghostly
Goosestep echoing
Through the young globe of her head.

And then the exit clearly
Marked 'Uitgang'
In the same blood colour
As Garbo's lips.

Outside the door, the canal
Flowed silent as the Styx.

Solution

So unlike school
This new examination hall:
Instead of Latin motto and crest,
A deformed crowfoot swastika;
Instead of teachers flexing canes,
Rifle butts against the spine;
Instead of portraits of a pompous head,
Blown-up photos of a neat
Little man with flustered face
And comical moustache.
And the question is more typical
Of playground riddles.
Anyone can tell
How 'dog' and 'fox' and 'field'
Can link into a sentence chain:
'The dog and fox are playing
In the field.' I must have
Passed. So why are soldiers shoving
Me inside the nightmare
Train? And why, instead of stars
On my report, does the engine
Spit gross constellations?

Flashback

Itaku-Shima,
The goddess Benten's
'Island of Light',
Gave Hiroshima
Its fame until
That morning
At eight fifteen.

Children were playing
Samurai with wooden
Swords and shields,
And flying dragon
Kites against
The sun, imagining
Them snort

Exotic flame.
Then a 'noiseless
Flash' slashed
The belly of sky
From east to west.
Bad light
Stopped play.

In The Blood Red

And when the war is over
Let's pretend it's not the end
And extend the wartime budget
By the days and months and years
That children were deprived of play
And widows stanched their tears.

Let's continue to send 'planes
But alter aims:
Instead of bombs,
Let us blitz with bread;
Instead of bullets,
Let us shoot with needles
That kill disease;
Instead of bayonets,
Let us cure with scalpels,
Lance the cataracts of the blind;
Instead of mines,
Let us plant
Maize and wheat and rice
To explode in harvest colours
Waving the flag we all recognise.

Our best intentions
Cannot raise the dead
But we can ply hope ladders
Of dollars, Deutschmarks, pounds,
And try to rescue balance sheets
Deep in the blood red.

Fishermen

With a needle's instinct for magnetic
North, the eye bagatelles
The corners of the frame, spins
Round the central circle
Of light and rests on the fishing
Boat's flickering flame.
A cyclops moon peeps
Out behind fingers of cloud,
Spotlighting the deep
Green lens of waves

Lancing the darkness

Until the deck is gleaming
With its silver hoard;
And lancing our cataracts,
Telescoping the second boat,
The corks, the gulls, the vague
Trees ghosting on the shore,
The anchor line, the painting's
Hair-thin cracks to cast
As nets on hidden shoals
Lit, like the fisherman's
Lamp, by a palette of oils.

The Barbara Hepworth Museum

In the green sub-tropical
Garden, in the clear St. Ives'
Neo-Florentine light,

Sculptures blossom with palms
And bamboo. Unburdened
By inscriptions to the dead,

Her monuments commemorate
The birthing of ideas; her
Universal language

Rinsing like a shower, sea
Spittle peeling cataracts
Of the day-to-day. The children's

Triptych washing
No longer hangs
In the marble yard; they grew

And flew like Atlantic gulls.
But the rest of her jungle 'jumble'
Breathes: the rocks, the sculptures,

Trees and flowers. Bronzes
Grow fresher every
Spring. Touch their skin

And you feel her pulse pacing
Contours of the Yorkshire dales.
The breeze plectrums her fingers—

With-strings; plays flautist
Through the hollows of her feminine forms.
And if someone were to fell

A limestone carving,
Rings would sing
The secrets of its age.

Piano Tuner

The blind piano tuner
Called twice yearly:

A mystical figure refusing
Lifts by car. Familiar

With pedals, warping wood,
The room's humidity, he seemed

A keyboard Casanova
Fingering each contour

With a touch approaching love.
Attentive to her scales, he showed

No disapproval at slack notes
But tapped his tuning fork

Then wound each key
To perfect and consistent pitch.

On off-key days
I envy the piano, long

For the tap-tap consolation
Of a blind man's step,

The magical vibration of his wand.

Asking David

Turning the pages,
His fingers trembled
Like trees in a Welsh
Wind. But when he read,
Seats assumed
The grain of chapel
Pews, the rostrum
Was his pulpit,
His Perrier water
Sparkled like the grail,
And words fell
Solid as if hewn
On tablets of stone.

Sharing his secrets,
He named the Artist
Who colours eternal
Skies; revealed
A score to resurrect
The carcases of song;
Etched luminous
Lines for nights
When our pits implode
And souls crawl,
Lampless, antennae
Frantic for light
And air seeping
From the hillside's wound.

After amens of applause,
Proferring my book,
His words,
Was asking David
To sign his psalms.

Then exits opened
Like breaks in cloud.
We followed
The moonlit river,
Less silted now,
To rooms less stranded,
To beds less bleak;
And wondered how
He crushed that nail,
The colour of ink,
The colour of pain.

Don Marcelino's Daughter

Bears made the first scratch,
Sharpening calcium razors
On caves' blank walls. That

Was before Don Marcelino's
Daughter crawled through the crevice
And held her incredulous candle

To the dying bison's eye.
Her own eyes danced
At every picture in the gallery:

Bulls, cows, prancing calves;
Their red coats sticking
To her finger. And the roof

Thundered with wild boars
And the unshod gallop
Of horses. I pictured

Her in the underpass
Watching vagrants chalk
Their memory of stallions

On cement: the trains' wheels
Clanking above; the draught
Extinguishing her candle.

(The Spanish nobleman, Don Marcelino de Sautuola,
excavated the Altamira cave at the foot of the Cantabrian
Hills in 1869. The quality of the Late Ice Age paintings
found there caused a revolution in prehistoric research.)

Off Broadway

After the champagne party,
The real pain began.

The midnight fingers
Of reviews
Extinguished all the bulbs
About her mirror,
Folded the show like costumes,
Quenched her jewelry
In the theatre safe.
Her wardrobe heart
Was emptied;
The letters of her name

Stripped from the stars
On her dressing room door.

The Purple Emperor

The Purple Emperor is the one
With a three-inch brilliance of wing span
Rising like flame to the highest
Oak leaves to feast on honeydew

The elusive butterfly who is tempted down
Not by flowers but by carrion
The flickering glory of the wood content
To sip the juice from excrement

Nests

Outside the bedroom window
A streetlight broke, and starlings

Gambled with the chip in the shade.
Their luck was in. Winnings

Of gold straw piled, and the nest
Eggs grew to healthy fledglings.

Behind the house, a different hand
Was dealt. Other starlings, deceived

By drought, built beneath the eaves,
Hatched, and proudly fed their young

Until flashfloods swept both
Nest and its raw hunger

Down the gutter's sudden rapids.
Frantic with instinct, they circled and flapped,

Fed worms to neighbour sparrows
In a ritual of expiation.

Lamprey

Wound escapes
The nightmare, refuses
To be canned. Wriggling
Through rushes, rocks

And riverbeds of dream,
It swims to my window
Each morning; fishpout
Rubbering glass.

Not lacerated,
Not breaking skin
To speak its pain,
This wound angles,

Plays the target,
Circles like a noose,
Triggers its
Strike: a lamprey's

Bloodshot snout
Clamping the flank
Of a passing trout,
Rasping flesh

And eating it alive,
Releasing a stain
Rinsed by sunset
Or evening rain.

'Clintona'

The children's heads were heavy
Like day-old
Colts', their bodies flabby,

Their lower lips protruding
In a pout. Some
Wore glasses; some clutched

Limbs limp as branches
Under snow.
But every child in the 'Clintona'

Coach seemed happy:
A certain symptom
I am told. A girl stumbled

Home on unsteady legs
And the driver stood
Alert as a stallion until

She reached the gate. In the back
Seat, a boy
Watched the magical designs

Of frost crystals on window
Panes, intent
As a geneticist detecting

The chromosome
In cells that spell,
At best, a life sentence.

Vicious Circle

Watching winos bent
Like broken springs
On the Circle Line
Platform, empty
Bottles rocking
At their feet, she recalls
The flowers, the laughter
And the song
Of another time
And whispers, 'Son,
They have no water.'

Old Coins

Precious few are treasured.
Most watch the currency of self
Devalue year by year, know
That they roll helpless

Down inflation's slope.
Some reopen letters
To confirm a life, turn
The albums' pages, sit

Before the T.V. screen,
Slide between cushions
Like loose change. A handful
Spend themselves in one

Last gamble. A few climb
Roofs, trailing meteoric
Glory in their fall, or balance
On a bridge before the electric leap

From world to world: a brilliance
Of coins in the fountain's cold
Bed welding mosaics
Of wishes unfulfilled.

Time Zones

The downstairs clock strikes every
Quarter hour, chiming its gentle parody
Of Big Ben; reminding me of London
And, earlier still, the three threes and a nine

Of Limerick's ubiquitous angelus bells
Calling us from play to six o'clock tea.
My mother kept the clock five minutes
Fast. Now she is five hours ahead

Sitting down alone to evening meals,
Receptive to echoes of that distant pealing.
Moving stiffly from chair to bed,
She is far too many hours ahead.

'Corrections'

When essays were returned,
We skipped two lines,
Highlighted 'Corrections'
With pared magenta pencils
And wrote the proper spelling,
Syntax, grammar . . . down
As if in expiation.

Later, we changed the jobs,
The cars, the houses, even wives;
Everything on which we felt
Perhaps we could improve.

Page after page,
We made the alterations
In our neatest hand
Until fading vision
Made errors hard to spot,
Harder to correct,
As calendar leaves yellowed and fell.

Like classroom ink
In which we dipped our brilliant nibs,
The sap of options dried.
Magenta pencils lost their point.

Slippers

Resting the long day's legacy
Of swollen feet in slippers softly
Contoured by bunions, corns, cramped

Toes – unique as fingerprints on glass –

She reads a Cinderella tale
To her granddaughter; eyes
Dancing across polished pages.

Bridget

Last of a breed, she rented the last mud floor
And open door. For eighteen years her voice
Was widow-soft and even less in tune
With time than the chapel's angelus bell.

Her place was by the fire. There on a smokey
Mantelpiece, the clock lay on its face.
A shallow grave of hands received her cheeks
Washed with the purgatorial tears of loss.

The fire was her companion though it lacked
A husband's heat to reach and warm the core
Of her tired heart. Sometimes its gaze transferred
A surface glow when flame-framed images

Recaptured flashing eyes, and reddening coals
Were blushes on the cheeks of her spent youth.
Then she had gripped wild ponies by the mane
And skipped and sung in flowers and freshening rain.

But joy remembered is not joy restored
And blazing thoughts increased the inner chill.
The pyre consumed her holocaust of dreams
And faith transported her to Calvary's hill.

Time did not gallop like the ponies of youth.
Instead, it roared impersonally by,
Jet engined. Childless, she sat in smoke beneath
Black sagging bags of canvas ceiling: sealing.

A Parting Gift

His friends made certain
That his nails remained uncut,
Then placed a harp beside him

As others had placed flowers.
'Just a little gesture,' they said,
Fixing the lid on the box,

'A parting gift to keep
The spirit strumming
If the church hasn't got it right

About the second coming.'
The wood was cut, shaped,
Planed from wild, eclectic

Memories of childhood;
Knotted and grained
With carols and party songs;

The strings woven
From hairs of every
Woman that his heart

Had loved, and the sound–
Chest resonant
With children's laughter.

If you walk among his favourite
Hills on a stormless night,
Glissando and arpeggio sounds

Will lead you to where
He lies – nails still uncut
And hard as diamonds.

A Bar of Soap

The small white bar was oblong,
Marble-smooth, grained, planed
And polished like a toy coffin.

Perhaps it was the silence of the room,
The stopped watch, beetles tanking
The no-man's land of unpolished
Boards, rats rustling across rafters,
The spider winding bluebottles
In sheets of lace, the damp air
Heavy as clay. Whatever; I knew
The hotel corridor fermented
With dead leaves and its lights were stars
And moon shafting through skeletal
Branches of yew. The warm soap
Comforted my fingers like a breast
And water rinsed and splashed: a silver,
Proselytising tongue, preaching

From its Jordan basin that death
Gives definition, cataracts life,
Teases the dirt from under its nails.

The Funeral Photographs

She too wants souvenirs of love,
    The 'other woman' hollow with grief
    And branded immoral, a thieving
Opportunist, though the jewel removed

Took little prising from complacent
    Claws. She asked for funeral
    Photos to compensate for all
The wedding snaps she never had. Quaint

Perhaps, but interesting to contrast
    Congratulations'
    Kiss with compassion's
Handshake, smile with tear, dress

With coat, bouquet with wreath. The coffin
    Is her favourite, her jewel
    Returned to earth, his final
Setting brilliant with the sinking sun.

Bequest

The sun does not die intestate.
It bequeaths the moon
And a tango of stars. My grandfather

Knew this because wisdom shines
Clear through the windows
Of a terminal ward and, aware

Of darkness congealing at the door,
He gathered light
And the half light. When the day nurse

Giggled on the telephone, he snatched
The sun and rolled
It under his bed. When the night nurse

Stole a minute's sleep,
He stuffed his pillow
With the moon: and when at last

He rested beyond sleep, they cleared
His locker and found
A bagful of stars. The sky

Is darker now but, contrary
To what the lawyers state,
He did not die intestate.

Pentecosts
(for Lynn)

When he said, 'Let there be light!'
And nothing happened, he knocked
The stone wall down and built
A wall of sheer translucent glass.

And, through the glass, they admired
The changing skies, the waders, reeds
And trees, the river ferrying sunlight
Under a stork-legged viaduct.

Together they saw that it was good
Until the slipping of her hand
From his, the fading of her face, her
Voice. He knew the waiting of those lost

Apostles in the upper room. No gales,
Of course, no tongues of fire.
But every day the little pentecosts,
Her wingbeat warm against his cheek.

Phoenix

The phoenix rises,
Clears his throat, grips
Between his talons, the body, nest
And ashes of his father, spreads
His gold-red wings

Towards Heliopolis and the altar
Of the sun. But windows, doors
And skylight are all barred.
He contemplates mahogany,
Calculates the span of half

A thousand years, accepts
There are no spice-trees
To construct a nest, settles
On the ashtray, begs
The chairman for a light.